I0163568

Simple Complex Shapes

Simple Complex Shapes

Vahni Capildeo

Shearsman Books

First published in the United Kingdom in 2015 by
Shearsman Books
50 Westons Hill Drive
Emersons Green
BRISTOL
BS16 7DF

Shearsman Books Ltd Registered Office
30–31 St. James Place, Mangotsfield, Bristol BS16 9JB
(this address not for correspondence)

www.shearsman.com

ISBN 978-1-84861-451-2

Copyright © Vahni Capildeo 2015

The right of Vahni Capildeo to be identified as the author of this work
has been asserted by her in accordance with the Copyrights,
Designs and Patents Act of 1988. All rights reserved.

For Gemma Robinson

enter me
inthedarkpleas
e so.only.see.
your.eyes.only.
feel.your.scars
up against my walls

Take her by the hand,
by the hair,
shut your eyes and lead her
to the sea
for the great ceremony of presentation:
the pinhead
where, if she's to dance,
she'll enjoy horizons.

       x

These warm trees,
they have intentions.
Make contact with them,
please, be flexible,
wash out your mouth with
dirt. And bark.

       x

eyes

      call to find out if to call

lips

      don't touch
      upon
      the touch
      of throats

hands

      in hotter climates
      trees shed leaves
      caravels and barques

They had words.
There were words between them.
They had words with each other.
How they wrote:
first, without signature;
then initialled;
names that bring strangeness,
that could bring about vows.
How they wrote to each other.
And these words
overwintered,
the words they had with each other;
these words
forced inwards
hyacinthine earstoppers,
makeless,
a pair.

Inconvenient body,
I awoke to you
and, like an architect
mad for steel and glass,
clad you, raked you high –
one prize fits all –
moved out

Discalendar this case,
aztecally: heart removals,
no sender
no return
no via dhl –
you've plateaued out,
zigzag – it's happening,
not lost,
between your eyes,
quetzalcoatl mon amour

Lord, should've noticed
you're my outstanding
biometric scanner failure

ten years plus
iris colour unknown

shining, their colour
is shining, lord

this river
beloved
whatever
grows because
prisoners
because
clunch fingers
because ducks
detailing
reeds bed down
like things mean
something slow
like this means
and it does
what you do
éventail
eventual
à cheval
adventure
nuit daylike
moth à moth
clé documents
kings' jews
safeguards running
éperdus
castled runes
clairière
outfoxed
clear
the air
challenges
simplicity
honey versions
hungry stones

```
                    why
        o            f         so
      those          l        yellow
                     o
                     w
                     e
                     r
                     s
        set                 rosettes
      thisisconsideredcreatingthegrounds
```

thing of air
our bond is water
equally any
land

don't let me go
don't go
do
don't let go

thing of air
our bond is water
around compounding
land

paid hands wet nape
exposed brickwork
look
this is tending

thing of air
our bond is water
dusted inside
land

lash flap slam streak
leopardcats exit
extend purr prank
attend

thing of air
our bond is water
overflowing flown
land

when
to be
was
to be going
and
having arrived
was
a small bird
then
to be going
was
no desirable
destination
what changed
you
desirable
as a destination
why
is this
now
where we were
become
that place
where
you are not
hillside
species recollected
above
bright clouds

this: when waking,
once awake, aware
that you exist,
waking, do not
speak or move;
so, leaving, gone,
go towards where
you are not;
reaching, find finding
elsewhere your somewhere
also; so loving
solitude in you,
in you love
your solitude: this
solitude means you.

now: if human
enough, directed through
museums of humanity,
human to you,
your soft plinth,
which body emits
warmth, which creates
a staircase of
its tallness, while
some slam doors;
fearing continuance: now
being aware, going
towards your solitude,
love, through bodies,
ironwork, acanthus blooms:

who's
sending you
on this mission:
tell her a story
a story to end today
in which she does not feature
in which she may be the character
heard singing in the woods – in which she is
that character; and since the men swanned off,
smoke nonetheless has been witnessed rising from over
the site of the old forge; make her
part of this story only if she
lives far from the woods and cannot
walk alone; if her beheaded
people have moved outside
books; if weapons
are mythopoetic,
self-funding

in my house
falling
through the floor
of myself
falling from falling in a father's house
from
the double attic
where wasps nested
cemented to beams
rosettes,
buttonholes, rugby balls
falling through floor
through ceiling falling
through ceiling floor
i cannot remember
how much further
there is
how this house
suffering from subsidence
presents
so many floors
i am solitaire
am the pack
reshuffled to make
a paper house
am the ground
recanting
tilted atop
a water course
this was
our house
a rooftree
the tiles roosting
and hospitable

there
the sky signs
who is missing
i take
the sun

Rain is falling gently on a sloping roof.
How am I to stay awake?

Leopardcats petition for their morning meats,
piteous, round-mouthed.

Look for them till you no longer
look at them. Bright sky.

They could not make a home with you
nor wait at home for you;

always they go home in you,
every happy solitude.

Solid rain. The metal roof
wavers. Gutters flute.
Paper boats rest quietly
within the house. Night's
tail-end, drawing over birds,
mutes their quirks. Quite tall
trees make sounds lost to rainfall,
quitting and yielding
different forms of breathing.
Now
water boiled last night,
cooled, poured into a jug, brings
human hands to play;
dawn
also, surveillance aircraft,
parrots, tourist jets,
sudden and gradual breaks
to a changeless state
where migrant writers find
their two-month home, strange fish
align with ice in markets.

knowing this
anti-escapologist
swallows his
own ropes

silence: cool water:
location of a thirst
i do not have
so far, so long as
i don't know
how pyramidal, how unmortared
i am built of
thirst, blocked in dust,
so outwith expectation
cool water:

glimpse – through water lightly held
in shape by glass as movement,
gleam and space for bright safe life;
say, fish scaling indifference,
signifying lateral
and easeful trails through silence –
each other, it is not time
that stops – well, what then – desire
rests in effigy until
some speech, love, some nightingale
begins, listeners still
fearing the dark, its kindness,
its definite discoveries

You have the same name as him.
My conscript tongue has practice
in bitter acrobatics,
transitioning from close to
close so often
to containment;
instead of climbing
those chained sounds that mean him, self-
saboteur, swallows
state-of-the-art equipment,
drops calls, lacerates greetings,
slides into appeal,
nylon misdirections, all to fall
into the place of amputation
he nominated mildness.
His name is to his palate.
It behaves.
Will not be severed from him.
You have the same name.
Yet for how many times it was his
in my mouth, it is yours once,
is the only sweet almond
in the tumbled bag,
is the spit buds taste.
For it has nothing of summoning,
your name: the mouth-bearing thing
I was, when shut up,
you so quickly translate
out of relation.
My tongue a blindfold
drawn by you finds you,
finding with each space that comes
it is coming in your shape.

```
            insist
this poem   IS           his poem
nocent                   innocent
knowing     FUN          spontaneous
            desist
            ex-
            re-
            sub-
```

i'm not your –	don't	pain ~~static~~
did i say –	pick	relation to pain ~~static~~
put that down –	things	relation to self ~~static~~
i'm not your –	out	relation to self as some-
		one in pain ~~static~~
why am i –	of	do we have enough
you know you –	a	~~words for a workshop~~
what are you	box	~~blood in us~~
being now? two	or	~~writing prompts~~
a.m. if only	roll	heating on?
more people usually	dice	vide cor meum

landing at night taut as pipework take pity as an aftertaste of waking in those persons whose position lets them normally sleep well and guide me quickly out of their sight for what's the point till i can make our point sharp as need be and go repeat go out of the dark

t-   -the
          RAW
1   x   tree
=   2   X

                    sai-
           l   nai- l
       l   l   l   l   l   l   l   l   l
     l   l   l   l   l   l   l   l   l   l   l
   l   l   l   l   l   l   l   l   l   l   l   l   l
                    a
                    a
                    a
                   real
                  harbour
                  hardest
                arborescent
                   -dour

lionfaced
kiss-request
mute
foot

hold on: if knots have names
no knot known here's named for
a swallow's head. remains
what part of desert lit
by wind, never by sun?
microscopic, hidden
even unto dust, some
labyrinth, some challenge
some physicist teased out
and said my god. hold on:
a bundle for a bed
darkbright winding up
reversible silver
thread. it was not the first
time ariadne took
the horned one for a walk,
undercover monster,
volunteer adventure
caving. tune out. hold on:

cold when you go into it
colder when you are gone from it
coldest from your being in it
what do you get out of it
this linen moon this upside bed
while the delicate pipeworked
gas tank stalls on the garage wall

a twist
there
as the crow lies,
the stoned crow, ground dove,
siskin, blue-grey tanager, attired
& emotional – a bit ropey,
tight between the teeth if – taught
enough to want/to re-use – reduce
first & sew realizing unless – spit,
draw the hanging end down;
there'll be no knot – not being knotted
at the outset, only holding on taut,
since when therefore
stubborn
gentle
irrelevance
become
resistant – oilslick plumage
epithets: denier of ribbons,
fence of birdsong,
time's autopilot,
long
sleep

~~love~~ ~~love~~ ~~love~~ ~~love~~ ~~love~~ ~~love~~
~~love~~ ~~moves~~ ~~moves~~ ~~moves~~ ~~love~~
~~love~~ ~~moves~~ this ~~moves~~ ~~love~~
~~love~~ ~~moves~~ ~~moves~~ ~~moves~~ ~~love~~
~~love~~ ~~love~~ ~~love~~ ~~love~~ ~~love~~ ~~love~~

www.ingramcontent.com/pod-product-compliance
Lightning Source LLC
Chambersburg PA
CBHW021947040426
42448CB00008B/1284